Collins English Readers

Amazing Performers

Level 1
CEF A2

Text by
Silvia Tiberio

Series edited by
Fiona MacKenzie

Collins

HarperCollins Publishers
77–85 Fulham Palace Road
Hammersmith London W6 8JB

10 9 8 7 6 5 4 3 2 1

ISBN: 978-0-00-754508-7

www.collinselt.com

A catalogue record for this book is available from the British Library

Printed in the UK by Martins the Printers

◆ Contents ◆

• Introduction •

Collins Amazing People Readers are collections of short stories. Each book presents the life story of five or six people whose lives and achievements have made a difference to our world today. The stories are carefully graded to ensure that you, the reader, will both enjoy and benefit from your reading experience.

You can choose to enjoy the book from start to finish or to dip into your favourite story straight away. Each story is entirely independent.

After every story a short timeline brings together the most important events in each person's life into one short report. The timeline is a useful tool for revision purposes.

Words which are above the required reading level are underlined the first time they appear in each story. All underlined words are defined in the glossary at the back of the book. Levels 1 and 2 take their definitions from the *Collins COBUILD Essential English Dictionary* and levels 3 and 4 from the *Collins COBUILD Advanced English Dictionary.*

To support both teachers and learners, additional materials are available online at www.collinselt.com/readers.

The Amazing People Club®

Collins Amazing People Readers are adaptations of original texts published by The Amazing People Club. The Amazing People Club is an educational publishing house. It was founded in 2006 by educational psychologist and management leader Dr Charles Margerison and publishes books, eBooks, audio books, iBooks and video content, which bring readers 'face to face' with many of the world's most inspiring and influential characters from the fields of art, science, music, politics, medicine and business.

♦ The Grading Scheme ♦

The Collins COBUILD Grading Scheme has been created using the most up-to-date language usage information available today. Each level is guided by a brand new comprehensive grammar and vocabulary framework, ensuring that the series will perfectly match readers' abilities.

		CEF band	Pages	Word count	Headwords
Level 1	elementary	A2	64	5,000–8,000	approx. 700
Level 2	pre-intermediate	A2–B1	80	8,000–11,000	approx. 900
Level 3	intermediate	B1	96	11,000–15,000	approx. 1,100
Level 4	upper intermediate	B2	112	15,000–19,000	approx. 1,700

For more information on the Collins COBUILD Grading Scheme, including a full list of the grammar structures found at each level, go to www.collinselt.com/readers/gradingscheme.

Also available online: Make sure that you are reading at the right level by checking your level on our website (www.collinselt.com/readers/levelcheck).

Glenn Miller

◆ ◆ ◆

1904–1944

the leader of the most famous big band in the USA

I was 11 years old when I used my money to buy my first instrument. I later formed an orchestra and created a new type of music. People enjoyed it so much! I played it for them until the end of my life.

◆ ◆ ◆

I was born in Clarinda, a small town in the state of Iowa in the United States on 1st March 1904. My parents had a small farm there. They didn't earn much money, but they worked really hard.

Our life was very quiet. Our farm was far away from other houses. In the summer, you could see miles of yellow fields from our home. In the winter, the same fields were often white with snow. Our life became quieter then. I went to school every day. I also worked on the farm. My parents paid me for my work, so I started to save some money. In my free time, I hit objects and listened to the sounds they made. I tried different types of objects and created new rhythms. It was fun.

◆ ◆ ◆

In 1915, when I was 11 years old, our family moved to Grand City in the state of Missouri. It was another very quiet town. At school, life was busy and I learned to play several instruments. Outside school, there wasn't much to do, so I found a way of spending my time. I used my money to buy a trombone and I played it in my free time. One day, I was asked to become a member of the local band. It was a very exciting time.

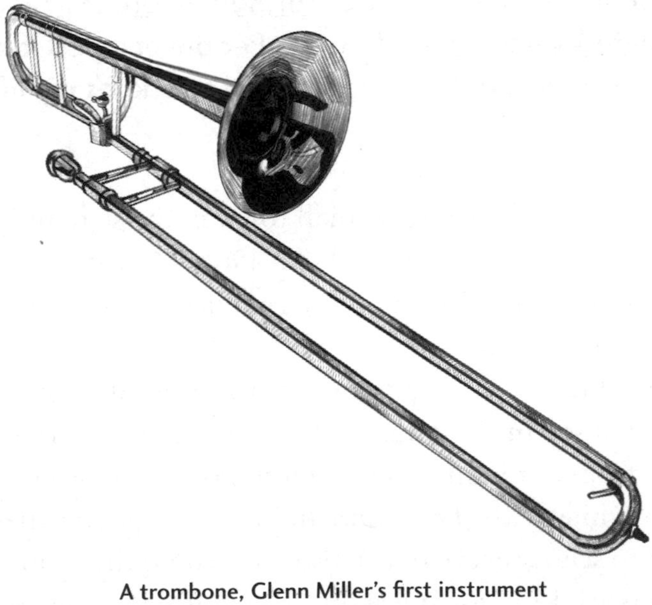

A trombone, Glenn Miller's first instrument

When my parents decided to move again in 1918, I was sad because I had to leave the band. We went to Fort Morgan, a small town in Colorado. Fort Morgan wasn't big, but it had a high school. And the school had a band! I was surprised. Soon, I was playing in a band again. I played the trumpet this time.

◆ ◆ ◆

When I finished high school in 1921, I had to choose the next step in my life. I liked to spend my time with people who liked music, so I joined Boyd Senter's band. But two years later, I decided to leave the band. I thought, 'I have to do a university course. It will help me to find a better job later in my life.'

I decided to attend the University of Colorado, but it wasn't a good decision. I went to bed late because I played in bands at night. I didn't do well because I didn't study hard. So I decided to leave the university.

◆ ◆ ◆

I had a dream – to become a professional musician and I told my parents about it. They listened to me and said, 'We're worried about your future. It isn't easy to earn money as a musician.' But I loved music and I decided to try.

My first step was to work with other musicians so I could learn from them. During this time, I wrote the first version of my first hit, *Moonlight Serenade*. This was the start of my career.

The next years were very busy. I moved to Los Angeles and joined Ben Pollack's band. After that, I travelled to New York and I played music in clubs at night. When I was in New York, I got married to Helen Burger, a girl I met at university. She didn't see much of me because I toured with bands and spent very little time at home.

I joined the Red Nichols Orchestra and played in several Broadway shows. I recorded some music and I also started to work with the Dorsey Brothers, a very popular band. 'Why are they so popular?' I asked myself. The answer was simple – their music was different from other types of music and it made people feel happy.

I spent a lot of time in theatres and studios. It was a happy time for me, but life was very hard for a lot of other people. There was a depression in the United States. A lot of people lost their jobs and they didn't have much money. They couldn't buy tickets for shows.

◆ ◆ ◆

In 1936, I was asked to appear in a film, *The Big Broadcast of 1936*. Great actors – Bing Crosby was one of them – also appeared in it. This film was very important in my career because it helped me to take a new, big step. I asked myself, 'Can I form my own band?' My answer was, 'Why not? I'm a good musician. I've worked with great bands. I have to try.'

So the next year, I formed my own band. People came to our shows and listened to our music. They danced and had fun. Our music was good, but I had a new idea now. I asked myself this time, 'Can I create a different type of music – a new special sound?' Once more, I decided to try. When Wilbur Schwartz, a great musician, joined my band, I told him about my idea. He liked the idea and we made a plan.

The main instruments of our band were a clarinet, three saxophones and a tenor saxophone – a saxophone that plays low sounds. Our music sounded really good. Our experiment worked! It was a new and different style.

Charlie Shribman, a businessman, liked our music. He told us, 'Your music is very good. I can organize a tour for you.' Soon we started our first tour and we played at the Glen Island Casino in 1939. The first night, 1,800 people came to listen to our music. It was a record at the time!

We recorded a lot of top hits. Adverts played our music on the radio and soon people knew our songs. One of our tunes, *Tuxedo Junction*, sold over 115,000 copies in a week. I also worked on films. One of them was *Sun Valley Serenade*. In this film, I played my song *Chattanooga Choo Choo*, which later sold 1.2 million copies! I was very busy, but I also wrote a book – *Glenn Miller's Method for Orchestral Arranging*.

I was very excited about my successful career, but the world was at war. The Germans were invading countries in Europe, and Japan and Germany were fighting together. The United States joined the war in 1941, when the Japanese attacked Pearl Harbor, an American port in Hawaii.

I wanted to help my country, but I couldn't join the army because I was 38 years old. I felt young and strong, but the soldiers in the army were much younger than me.

I was very upset because I really wanted to help. I thought, 'Could I be in charge of an army band?' I wrote a letter to Brigadier General Charles Young, an important official in the army. He liked my idea and soon I was in charge of a small band in Alabama. We played music to the soldiers. We also played music during parades.

Everyone in the army liked our music. It was good for the soldiers because it helped them to feel happy in difficult times. Soon I was allowed to form a new, bigger band. It had 50 musicians. It was the Army Air Force Band.

In 1944, there were many American soldiers in Britain because they were getting ready to fight the Germans. In the summer, I was asked to take the band to England. And on 15th December that same year, I was asked to go to Paris to play for the soldiers who were there.

It was my last flight. The plane disappeared over the English Channel. What was the reason for the accident? Was it a bomb? Was it bad weather? No one ever knew. The Second World War destroyed the dreams of millions of people. It also destroyed mine.

The Life of Glenn Miller

1904 Alton Glenn Miller was born on a farm in Clarinda, Iowa, USA.

1915 His family moved to Grand City in Missouri. Glenn started to play the trombone.

1918 His family moved to Fort Morgan in Colorado. Glenn joined his new high school's band.

1921 He finished high school and joined the Boyd Senter band. It was the first musical group that he joined.

1923 He left the band to go to the University of Colorado. He left university to become a musician.

1926 He travelled to Los Angeles and joined Ben Pollack's band.

1928 Glenn moved to New York. He married Helen Burger, a girl he met at university. Over the next few years, he joined the Red Nichols Orchestra and worked with the Dorsey Brothers.

1934 He made his first recording.

1936 Glenn worked on the film *The Big Broadcast of 1936.*

1937 He formed his own band.

1938 He created a special sound for the band. He recorded with RCA Victor Records.

1939 Glenn and his band played at the Glen Island Casino. For the next four years, the Glenn Miller Orchestra became very popular. They recorded 70 top ten hits, for example, *Moonlight Serenade* and *In the Mood.*

1941 The United States joined the Second World War. Glenn made his first Twentieth Century Fox film, *Sun Valley Serenade.*

1942 Glenn joined the US Army Air Force. He formed the Glenn Miller Army Air Force Band.

1944 On 15th December, Glenn was on a flight to Paris. The plane disappeared over the English Channel.

Pérez Prado

1916–1989

the Cuban musician who was known as 'the King of Mambo'

When I was a child, I enjoyed the rhythm of different types of music. I learned to play the piano and soon I had a band. We played Latin dance music. People listened to our music in different parts of the world!

◆ ◆ ◆

I was born in a small town in Cuba on 11th December 1916. I was always interested in music. When I was a child, I liked to listen to different types of music and compare their rhythms. 'Why is music from Mexico different from music from France? Why is music by Bach different from music by Gershwin?' I often thought.

My country's music was different from all of the other types of music that I knew. In Cuba, there were a lot of African people. When they came from Africa, they brought their music with them. Our music was special because it was a mixture of Latin music and African music.

My father worked for a newspaper. My mother was a school teacher and she wanted me to learn. I had a talent for music, so one day, they told me, 'You should take lessons.' I liked the idea. First, I studied the piano and then, I learned to play the organ. I enjoyed my music lessons. I studied hard and practised a lot because I wanted to be a good musician. When I was a teenager, I could play both the piano and the organ really well.

⬩ ◆ ⬩

Soon I had my first job – I played music at local clubs. And next, I played music professionally. I became the pianist of Cuba's most popular group, Sonora Matancera, and I also arranged their songs. We played mambos, tangos and other types of Latin music. I also became a member of the Orquesta Casino de la Playa, Cuba's most important orchestra. I lived in Cuba's capital city, Havana, during this time.

In 1948, I moved to Mexico and formed my own band. We played mambo because it was my favourite type of music. It had good rhythm and people enjoyed dancing to it. In the same year, I signed a contract with a company called RCA Victor and I recorded my music for the first time. In 1949, I recorded a very popular song, *Mambo Number 5*. The next year, I recorded *Qué Rico el Mambo* and it went to the top of the charts.

One day in 1950, Sonny Burke, an American producer, heard my music when he was on holiday in Mexico. He

A couple dancing the mambo

asked me to record *Qué Rico el Mambo* in the USA! He gave it a new name, *Mambo Jambo*, and it became a big hit. In the same year, I also recorded my first album, *Pérez Prado*. A new and exciting time began!

◆ ◆ ◆

In 1951, I was very busy. I moved my band to the USA and we toured the country with our music. It became very popular all over the country. I also started a family. I got married to Maria Engracia Salinas and we later had a son and a daughter.

In 1955, one of my songs, *Cherry Pink and Apple Blossom White*, got to number one in the charts. It was a French song that was in the Latin style. Next, there were many more hits. One of them was *Patricia*. People across the whole country were dancing to it!

◆ ◆ ◆

But in Cuba, things were very different. People were very poor and a group of men who were against the government started a revolution in 1959. Their leader was Fidel Castro and Che Guevara was the head of their army. They started a new political system – communism. In this system, there is no private property. People didn't own their homes and they couldn't listen to my music. Songs can give ideas to people, so the government didn't want people to listen to them. I felt very sad. My music was international, but I couldn't play it in my country!

In the USA, I noticed that people's interest in music was changing again. Rock and roll was heard in the streets and on the radio. A group, Bill Haley and the Comets, and a singer, Elvis Presley, were playing a new type of music. I was 45 years old and they were 20 years younger. I decided it was time to return to Mexico and spend more time with my wife and my two children.

I wanted to live a quiet life, but soon I was busy again. I received invitations from Japan and countries in South America. I toured these countries and played my music as people danced and danced. In 1987, I returned to the USA to give a final concert in New York. It was a happy time and a good way to say goodbye. Two years later, on 14th September 1989, I died.

The Life of Pérez Prado

1916 Pérez Prado was born on 11th December in Matanzas, Cuba. When he was a child, he learned to play the organ and the piano.

1936 He started to play the organ and the piano in local clubs. He became the pianist of Cuba's best known musical group, Sonora Matancera. He also arranged their songs.

1942 He moved to Havana.

1943 He joined Cuban's most important orchestra, Orquesta Casino de la Playa.

1947 He moved to Puerto Rico and toured with a group of musicians.

1948 The tour finished in Mexico City and he decided to stay there. He formed his own band. He signed a contract with RCA Victor and recorded his music for the first time.

1949 He recorded his hit song *Mambo Number 5.*

1950 Sonny Burke heard *Qué Rico el Mambo* while he was on holiday in Mexico. He asked Pérez Prado to record the song again as *Mambo Jambo.* It became a hit. Pérez recorded his first album, *Pérez Prado.*

1951 Pérez married Maria Engracia Salinas and they later had two children. He toured the USA and recorded more music.

1955 He changed the French song *Cherry Pink and Apple Blossom White* to Latin style. It got to number one in the American charts.

1958 His song *Patricia* got to number one in the charts. His music became international.

1970s He returned to Mexico and lived with his family. Pérez recorded more songs and toured Mexico, South America and Japan.

1987 He returned to the USA for a final concert at the Palladium Ballroom in New York. He also made his last recording. He became ill. His son became the new leader of his band.

1989 He died in Mexico City, Mexico on 14th September. He was 72 years old.

Ella Fitzgerald

1917–1996

the most popular female jazz singer in the USA

My mother was dead. I was alone and I lived on the streets of New York. I was a teenager and didn't have a home. My future was dark. But I became rich and won 14 Grammy Awards.

♦ ◆ ♦

I was born in Virginia in the United States on 25th April 1917. It was a difficult time for my mother because she lived alone with me. She had to look after me and she had to work to earn some money. She didn't have a good job.

I was only 3 years old when my mother decided to move to New York. Soon, I had a new home and a new family. I lived in Yonkers – a neighbourhood in New York – with my mother, my new half-sister and her father. While I lived in this neighbourhood, I made new friends and played with them in the street. My half-sister was called Frances and she was six years younger than me.

My mother had very little money, but she tried hard to give me a good education. She wanted me to have a better chance in life than her. 'Work hard at school,' she told me. And she often took me to church. The church had a choir and I liked their songs. When they invited me to join them, I was very excited. 'I want to have a career as a singer,' I thought.

At home, I always sang and danced while I listened to the radio. My mother looked at me and thought, 'Ella has a talent for music.' One day, she bought me some records by Connee Boswell, a great jazz singer. Her songs became my favourite songs and I practised them all day. I wanted to sing like her.

At school, I enjoyed the drama classes and I played different roles. My teachers wanted me to work hard on all the courses, but I only worked really hard on my drama course.

◆ ◆ ◆

One day, when I was 15 years old, my life changed suddenly. My mother had a heart attack and died. In the streets of New York, there was a lot of noise and traffic. At home, there was only silence. The radio didn't play music any more. My sister and I were both very sad. Aunt Virginia said to us, 'Why don't you come home and live with me?' She was a kind woman. She liked jazz music and she encouraged me to sing. But I wasn't happy at all.

I wanted to earn my own money. I started to miss school and when I was at school I didn't study very hard. I met people on the streets and they offered me jobs. I was young and I didn't have much experience of life. I didn't know that the jobs were dangerous. Soon, I got into trouble with the police and I was sent to a reform school – a school for children who get into trouble. I thought, 'Is this really happening to me?' I was very sad.

◆ ◆ ◆

I was at a reform school in a part of New York called The Bronx and then I was moved to another school in Hudson. I didn't like the students in the school – most of them were criminals. Life was very difficult and I escaped from the school. I was a teenager, I was alone and I didn't have a home. I lived on the streets of Harlem in New York.

Life on the streets wasn't easier than life at the reform school. I was hungry, I didn't have a job and I didn't have any money. But 21st November 1934 was my lucky day. There was a competition at the Apollo Theatre in Harlem and I went to see it with some friends. When I was there, I decided to take part in it. I went on stage and sang *Judy*, one of Connee Boswell's songs. Then I sang *The Object of my Affection*, a song by The Boswell Sisters. I sang well, but I was surprised by the result. I won first prize! This was the most exciting day of my life!

◆ ◆ ◆

After my performance at the Apollo Theatre, I started to be in contact with people in the music industry. One day, I met Chick Webb, a bandleader who needed a singer. My life changed again. The girl from the reform school was a singer in a band now!

In 1936, I made my first recording with Chick Webb and in 1938, I recorded *A-Tisket A-Tasket*. It sold one million copies, became a hit and stayed in the charts for 17 weeks. I turned on the radio and I heard my songs. I was 21 years old and I was a famous singer. For the first time in my life, I earned more money than I could spend in a day.

When Chick Webb died in 1939, I was asked to become the new bandleader. It was an important job and I didn't have much education. I had to learn the words and I had to arrange a lot of songs. There were many shows and my life was very busy.

⬥ ◆ ⬥

Two years later, in 1941, the United States entered the Second World War. As I sang my songs, I tried to make people feel happy. There weren't many shows during this time, but when the war ended in 1945, my life became busier than ever.

There were more and more shows. People liked my scat singing. This was a type of jazz singing – I sang sounds instead of words. I worked with great musicians. One of them was Norman Granz. First, I sang with his band and then, he became my manager.

A big sign for one of Ella's shows

Some of my songs, for example *Oh, Lady Be Good* and *How High the Moon*, became big hits. I toured for 40 or more weeks a year. I flew to Europe and visited great cities. I went to South America and learned about Latin music. I also went to Japan. My music was international! My name was in lights on big signs and I was a star! I won the National Medal of Arts and the Presidential Medal of Freedom. I also won 14 Grammy Awards – a prize that is given by the National Academy of Recording Arts and Sciences of the United States.

In 1985, I was 68 years old and I was ill. My heart was weak. I also had diabetes – there was too much sugar in my blood. The diabetes slowly affected different parts of my body. First, it affected one of my eyes and then it affected my legs. Both of them were amputated below the knee.

I spent the last years of my life in a wheelchair in my house in Beverly Hills near Los Angeles. I smelled the air and listened to the birds in my garden. I thought about my life and thanked God for my wonderful voice.

The Life of Ella Fitzgerald

1917 Ella Jane Fitzgerald was born in Newport News, Virginia, USA.

1920 Ella and her mother moved to Yonkers, New York.

1923 Ella's half sister, Frances Da Silva, was born.

1932 Ella's mother died from a heart attack. Ella went to live with her mother's sister but became unhappy. She escaped from reform school and lived on the streets of Harlem, New York.

1934 Ella took part in a competition at the Apollo Theatre in Harlem, New York. She won first prize.

1936 Ella made her first recording with Chick Webb, called *Love and Kisses.*

1938 Her song *A-Tisket A-Tasket* sold one million copies. It stayed in the charts for 17 weeks.

1939 Chick Webb died and Ella became the leader of his band.

1940 Ella was invited to sing in the Hollywood movie *Ride 'Em Cowboy.*

1941 She married Ben Kornegay. Her marriage ended after two years. The United States joined the Second World War.

1942 Ella left the band. She decided to begin her own career.

1945 The Second World War ended.

1948 She married Ray Brown.

1953 Ella's marriage to Ray Brown ended. She chose Norman Granz as her manager.

1958 She won her first Grammy Award for Best Jazz Individual Performance.

1972 Diabetes affected one of her eyes and she couldn't see out of it.

1987 She won the National Medal of Arts.

1988 She recorded for the last time.

1992 She won the Presidential Medal of Freedom.

1993 Both of Ella's legs were amputated.

1996 She died at her home near Los Angeles on 15th June. She was 79 years old.

Luciano Pavarotti

1935–2007

one of the world's best opera singers

My father sang very well and my mother and I enjoyed his beautiful songs. I played football very well and I wanted to become a famous footballer. But I became one of the greatest opera stars in the world instead!

◆ ◆ ◆

When I was born on 12th October 1935, my parents lived in a small house near the town of Modena in the north of Italy. My mother worked in a factory and my father worked in a bakery.

My father was a very good singer and his music brought happiness to our home. He often sang during breakfast before going to the bakery and then he sang again when he came home after work. He had a beautiful tenor voice. 'I hope you'll sing like your father,' my mother often said.

But one day, the happy times came to an end. I was only 4 years old when the Second World War started in 1939. At first, the war seemed very far away, but soon it began to get closer each day. Men left their jobs to join the army, so factories had only a few workers. At home, my mother had very little food to put on our plates.

Things got worse when, in 1943, we learned that we had to leave our house. Soldiers fought each other and planes dropped bombs very near our home. It was very dangerous to stay in our town, so we had to move to a nearby farm.

My father rented a small room on the farm. The room was made of stone and it was cold. My mother tried to make a home for us in this room, but it wasn't easy. My father didn't sing any more.

◆ ◆ ◆

We danced and celebrated when we learned that the war was over. We were very excited because we could move back to our home. Once we were in our town, my father started singing again. Our life was normal again. I went to school every day.

At school, I played football. I was a very good player. I was so good that I wanted to be a professional football player one day. At home, my father taught me several songs and we often sang them together. My father was a member of Corale Rossini Choir, the church choir.

One day, I went to the church with him and I sang in the choir. Most of the members of the choir were much older than me, but I didn't mind. I learned a lot from them.

◆ ◆ ◆

The most important experience of my life came next, in 1955. I can still remember it very clearly. My father said, 'We're going to be in an international competition for choirs. We're going to travel to a country called Wales – it's near England.' I didn't know much about Wales, but I asked, 'Where in Wales will it be?' 'In a small town called Llangollen,' my father answered. He couldn't pronounce Llangollen correctly. 'You should sing it,' I said. When my father sang, all words sounded good!

Everyone in the choir was excited about our trip to Llangollen. We bought new clothes because we needed a uniform. I got a map and found Llangollen on it and I took a passport, too. Soon, we were ready and we set off in a coach. The journey was long, but time passed quickly because we sang most of the way.

Llangollen was a lovely little town. We looked at its beautiful mountains and felt very happy. On the day of the competition, we sang really well. 'This was our best performance,' I thought. And it really was! The judge gave the result: 'The winner is Corale Rossini Choir!' We won first prize!

◆ ◆ ◆

On my way home, I thought about my future. I didn't want to be a professional football player any more. After I got home, I told my mother, 'I had a very good time in Llangollen. I want to become a professional singer.' I was excited but she looked worried. She didn't think it was a good idea. 'I think you should have a professional job,' she said.

My mother's opinion was very important for me, so I became a teacher and got a job in a school. But I decided to take singing lessons as well. My father knew an opera singer from our town. His name was Arrigo Pola and he taught me for three years. He didn't ask me to pay for his lessons because I had very little money. I learned a lot from him and I always remembered his help.

In 1957, Arrigo moved to Japan because he got a job at Tokyo University. But we often wrote to each other and I even travelled to Japan to visit him. This was a very interesting experience.

I now wanted to become a professional opera singer. I got some small jobs so that I could pay for my lessons. I sang in concerts, competitions and in some local opera houses. It was a busy time until one day the sound of my voice was strange. I couldn't sing very well, so I went to see a doctor. 'You have to rest your voice,' the doctor said. I was worried. Was this the end of my career?

◆ ◆ ◆

I rested my voice for some time. In 1961, I got married to Adua Veroni, an opera singer, and we started a family. I also had my first main role in an opera called *La Bohème.*

Important directors heard about me. One of them invited me to perform at the Vienna State Opera in Austria. Then, I was invited to sing at the Royal Opera House in London because the lead singer, Giuseppe di Stefano, became ill. After that, I toured Australia with Joan Sutherland, a great opera singer. We did over 40 performances in big cities and small towns of this wonderful country. And then, we toured the United States and I sang at the Greater Miami Opera. I enjoyed all these international tours but I also wanted to sing in my own country. Finally I did this, when, on 28th April 1965, I performed in La Scala, Milan's opera house.

La Scala Opera House, Milan, Italy

In 1966, at the Royal Opera House in London, I was able to sing nine high Cs – very high notes. At the Metropolitan Opera in New York, I also did a great performance and I took 17 curtain calls! The people clapped and I had to walk to the front of the stage 17 times!

I had more fans each day. I sold millions of copies of my albums and won a Grammy Award – a prize that is given by the National Academy of Recording Arts and Sciences of the United States.

I was very successful. But I also wanted to help other people. In 1982, I started the Pavarotti International Voice Competition for young singers. There were two more, in 1986 and 1989. I also helped charitable organizations.

In 1990, the Football World Cup took place in Italy and I was asked to sing during the opening ceremony. I sang *Nessun Dorma*, a song from *Turandot*, an opera by Giacomo Puccini. It became an international hit. It was played around the world and my name was heard in every country.

I was asked to do more and more international performances. My fans were often disappointed because I had to cancel some performances. I had to rest my voice. So, when I was asked to become a member of the group The Three Tenors, I was very pleased. The other members of the group were Plácido Domingo and José Carreras, two famous Spanish opera singers. It was good to sing with other people because my voice didn't have to do all the work in concerts. We performed in big cities around the world like Los Angeles, Paris and Tokyo.

But I also performed on my own. Between 1991 and 1993, I gave large concerts at Hyde Park in London, Central Park in New York and the Eiffel Tower in Paris. Hundreds of thousands of people came to listen to me. In New York, for example, more than half a million people were there to listen to me!

So much work and so many tours affected my family life. In 1995, after 34 years, my marriage ended.

In 2003, I got married to my assistant, Nicoletta Mantovani and the next year I started my last tour. I flew from one big city to another and visited 40 cities. Sometimes I didn't know which airport I was in. I performed for the last time in Italy in 2006.

A year later, I was given very sad news. The doctor said I had cancer. My life was coming to an end. I did charitable work and I thought about my past. I had so many happy moments. I had a long, exciting life.

The Life of Luciano Pavarotti

1935 Luciano Pavarotti was born in Modena, Italy on 12th October.

1943 During the Second World War, his family moved to the countryside.

1944 Luciano joined the church choir, Corale Rossini Choir. He was 9 years old.

1955 Corale Rossini Choir won first prize at an international competition in Llangollen, Wales.

1961 He married opera singer, Adua Veroni. They later had three daughters. He had his first main role in the opera *La Bohème* at the Teatro Municipale in Reggio Emilia, a city in the north of Italy.

1963 Luciano sang at the Vienna State Opera in Austria. He sang at the Royal Opera House in London. He went on an Australian tour with Joan Sutherland.

1965 He sang at the Greater Miami Opera in the United States. He also sang at La Scala, the opera house in Milan, Italy.

1966 At the Royal Opera House in London, he sang nine high Cs.

1972 At the Metropolitan Opera in New York, he took 17 curtain calls.

1977 He appeared in his first television performance, *Live from the Met*.

1990 Luciano sang *Nessun Dorma* at the 1990 Football World Cup. He formed The Three Tenors with Plácido Domingo and José Carreras. They gave a concert together in Rome. Their record sold more copies than any other classical record.

1993 Over half a million people went to listen to Luciano in New York's Central Park.

1994 He performed with The Three Tenors in Los Angeles, USA.

1995 His marriage to Adua Veroni ended.

1998 He received a Grammy Award. He performed with The Three Tenors in Paris, France.

2002 He performed with The Three Tenors in Japan.

2003 Luciano married Nicoletta Mantovani.

2004 He began his last tour. He was 69 years old.

2006 He gave his final performance of *Nessun Dorma* at the opening ceremony of the Winter Olympics in Turin, Italy.

2007 He died at his home in Modena, Italy on 6th September. He was 71 years old.

John Lennon

♦ ◆ ♦

1940–1980

member of the famous band The Beatles

When I was young, I failed all my exams. But I didn't worry. I had a guitar and I had a band. My band became the greatest band in the world.

♦ ◆ ♦

When I was born in England on 9th October 1940, a lot of countries were at war. It was the Second World War. I lived in the city of Liverpool. German bombs were destroying the city. It was dangerous to live there and it was a very sad time.

As a child and teenager, my life was difficult. My father worked on a ship and spent very little time in our house. In fact, he wasn't even in our country the day that I was born. My mother was alone most of the time. My father didn't send her much money and she had very little money to buy the things that we needed.

In 1944, my father didn't send us any more money. Aunt Mimi and her husband offered to look after me and I moved to their house. When my father came back, he argued with my mother. Then he said to me, 'I'm going to New Zealand. Would you like to come with me?' I agreed, but when my mother walked away, I started to cry. I couldn't live so far away from home. I was very young and I still needed my mother. So my father left and I stayed. But I didn't stay with my mother. I stayed with Aunt Mimi instead.

♦ ◆ ♦

My aunt and uncle were very kind to me. I liked music, so they bought me a mouth organ. It was my first musical instrument. I moved it across my lips and blew air through it. It was very small but I could create music with it! Then one day when my mother visited me, she brought a banjo – a type of small guitar – and she taught me how to play it. I liked to play musical instruments.

At school, the teachers didn't like me. I wasn't a quiet boy and I wasn't a good student. In one of my school reports, a teacher wrote that I was 'a clown in class' and that I wasted other pupils' time. When I was 16 years old, I failed all my exams. Aunt Mimi talked to me about my bad exam results. She was worried, but I wasn't. I wasn't interested in school work and I wasn't going to spend my time on it. I was interested in music and art.

Next, I started to study at the Liverpool College of Art. I also wanted to study music, but Aunt Mimi didn't think it was a good idea. I told my mother about my love for music and she lent me some money to buy a guitar. I could now form a band!

In 1957, I began classes at the college. I wore 'Teddy Boy' clothes – narrow trousers and a long jacket that were in fashion at the time. I didn't study much, I spent time playing music and I failed all my exams. I was asked to leave the college.

◆ ◆ ◆

Now I had more time to play music with my band. It was called The Quarrymen and we played skiffle music. Unusual objects, drums and guitars are used to play this type of music. I met Paul McCartney at our second performance and I asked him to join us. He was younger than me, but he was a great guitar player. We started writing songs together and we moved from skiffle music to rock and roll. Later, George Harrison and Ringo Starr joined us. Stuart Sutcliffe, a friend from art school, played the drums. We played a lot of American rock songs.

Life seemed happy, but it suddenly changed. On 15th July 1958, my mother was hit by a car and died. I was very sad. I didn't have a mother or a father now. Music helped me to feel better and Aunt Mimi helped me, too. But I needed to spend time with people of my own age. When Cynthia Powell became my girlfriend, I started to smile again.

As I played music, I thought about my band. 'Let's play our own music, not American songs,' I said to myself. We started writing and playing our own songs, and soon we became a popular group in Liverpool. Our band was different now, so we needed a new name. We changed it to The Beatles. In 1960, we signed a contract to sing for 48 days at a club in Germany.

◆ ◆ ◆

When we came back from Germany, we met Brian Epstein, a man who had a music shop. He liked our music and he offered to be our manager. He wanted 25 per cent of our gross income – the total amount of the group's earnings. We didn't know much about the business and we didn't have any other contracts, so we agreed.

And we made the right decision. Brian soon found a company that was interested in our songs. We signed our first contract and, on 6th June 1962, we recorded at the Abbey Road Studios. Our first song, *Love Me Do*, was played a lot on the radio. *Please Please Me*, our next song, went to the top of the charts. It was the start of a very busy life. I was married to Cynthia by now and I also had a son.

From 1963 to 1966, we travelled to several countries and we also wrote and recorded new songs. We lived in hotels, theatres and music studios. I also appeared on TV and in a film, *A Hard Day's Night*, which was successful. We were very famous and had a lot of fans. People stopped us on the streets!

◆ ◆ ◆

I knew how life could suddenly change and it happened once again. In 1967, Brian Epstein died and The Beatles didn't have a manager any more. In 1968, my marriage ended. Yoko Ono, a Japanese artist came into my life and, in 1969, I got married to her. The Beatles' music wasn't as popular as before. In 1970, Paul McCartney left the band. And, in 1971, I decided to leave England and move to the United States. I wanted to begin a new life.

In the United States, I lived in New York with Yoko most of the time. I wrote songs and recorded my own albums and albums with Yoko. I also started a record company and gave concerts. I was against the war in Vietnam and I expressed my ideas about peace in my songs *Give Peace a Chance, All You Need is Love, Imagine* and many others. President Nixon and other politicians didn't like my comments about war and they wanted to send me out of the country. I wasn't American, after all. Finally, in 1976, I was given permission to stay in the USA.

Imagine was one of my most popular songs. In this song, I say 'I'm a dreamer' and I really was one. I dreamed about peace and about love, but, on 8th December 1980, when I was walking into my apartment in New York, a man shot me with his gun. That was the end of my life.

Today, a lot of people listen to my songs and dream about peace and love. As I say in my song, 'I'm a dreamer, but I'm not the only one.'

The Life of John Lennon

1940 John Lennon was born in Liverpool, England.

1944 He went to live with his aunt and uncle.

1956 John's mother helped him to buy a guitar. He formed a band, The Quarrymen.

1957 Paul McCartney joined the band. John began classes at Liverpool College of Art.

1958 He wrote his first song, *Hello Little Girl.* George Harrison joined the band. His mother was killed in a car accident.

1960 The band changed its name to The Beatles. They signed a contract to perform in Germany.

1961 The band met Brian Epstein at Liverpool's Cavern Club.

1962 The band signed a contract with Brian Epstein. They recorded at the Abbey Road Studio. They recorded their first single, *Love Me Do.* John married Cynthia Powell.

1963 The band recorded *Please Please Me.* The group recorded their second album. John's son, Julian, was born.

1964 The Beatles began their first American tour. John's first book, *In His Own Write*, was published. John filmed the movie, *A Hard Day's Night*. The band recorded their third album, *A Hard Day's Night*.

1965 The Beatles movie, *Help!*, was filmed. The band played to a crowd of over 50,000 fans in New York.

1967 Brian Epstein died and The Beatles didn't have a manager any more.

1968 John's marriage to Cynthia Powell ended. He recorded his first album with Yoko Ono.

1969 The album *Yellow Submarine* was recorded. John married Yoko Ono.

1970 The Beatles recorded their final album, *Let It Be*. Paul McCartney left The Beatles. John recorded his own album, *Plastic Ono Band*.

1971 John moved to the United States. He recorded *Imagine* at his home studio.

1975 John and Yoko had a son.

1980 He recorded his last album, *Double Fantasy*. He was killed by Mark David Chapman on 8th December. He was 40 years old.

Glossary

affect VERB
to influence something or someone or cause them to change

amputate VERB
to remove someone's arm or leg in a surgical operation

arrange VERB
to change or adapt a piece of music so that it is suitable for particular instruments or voices, or for a particular performance

bakery NOUN
a place where bread and cakes are baked or sold

bandleader NOUN
the person who conducts a band, especially a jazz band

Broadway NOUN
an area of New York City where there are many theatres and many famous plays and shows are performed

cancel VERB
to say that something that has been planned will not happen

cancer NOUN
a serious disease that makes groups of cells in the body grow when they should not

career NOUN
a job that you do for a long time, or the years of your life that you spend working

ceremony NOUN
a formal event

charge
in charge of something PHRASE
to be responsible for something

charitable ADJECTIVE
helping and supporting people who are ill, disabled or poor

chart NOUN
the official list that shows which songs or records have sold the most copies each week

choir NOUN
a group of people who sing together

church NOUN
a building where Christians go to pray

clarinet NOUN
a musical instrument that you blow. It is a long, black, wooden tube with keys on it that you press and a single reed (= a small, flat part that moves and makes a sound when you blow).

clown NOUN
someone who says funny things or does silly things to amuse people

contract NOUN
an official agreement between two companies or two people

create VERB
to make something happen or exist

criminal NOUN
a person who does something illegal

depression NOUN
a time when there is very little economic activity so a lot of people do not have jobs

destroy VERB
to cause so much damage to something that it cannot be used any longer, or does not exist any longer

earnings PLURAL NOUN
the money that you earn by working

encourage VERB
to try to persuade someone to do something

form VERB
to start an organization

half-sister NOUN
a girl or woman who has either the same mother or the same father as you

heart attack NOUN
when someone suddenly has a lot of pain in their chest and their heart stops working

hit VERB
to touch someone or something with a lot of force
NOUN
a piece of music, film or play that is very popular and successful

industry NOUN
all the people and activities involved in making a particular product or providing a particular service

invade VERB
to attack and enter a country

judge NOUN
a person who decides who will be the winner of a competition

Latin ADJECTIVE
relating to countries in Latin America, for example Cuba, Puerto Rico, Argentina and Brazil

local ADJECTIVE
in, or relating to, the area where you live

mambo NOUN
a type of dance music originally from Cuba

marriage NOUN
the relationship between two people who are legally partners

narrow ADJECTIVE
small in distance from one side to the other

neighbourhood NOUN
one of the parts of a town where people live

note NOUN
one particular sound, or a symbol that represents this sound

official NOUN
a person who holds a position of power in an organization

orchestra NOUN
a large group of musicians who play different instruments together

organ NOUN
a large musical instrument that is like a piano

parade NOUN
a line of people or vehicles moving through a public place in order to celebrate an important event

peace NOUN
a situation where there is not a war

performance NOUN
when you entertain an audience by singing, dancing or acting

political ADJECTIVE
relating to politics or the government

port NOUN
a town by the sea where ships arrive and leave

producer NOUN
a person whose job is to produce plays, films, programmes or music

professional ADJECTIVE
doing an activity as a job rather than just for enjoyment

professionally ADVERB
in a way that involves doing something as a job, rather than just for enjoyment

property NOUN
buildings, land or other things that belong to a particular person

record VERB
to store something such as a musical performance on a disk so that it can be heard or seen again later
NOUN
1 the best result ever in a particular activity or sport
2 a round, flat piece of plastic on which sound, especially music, is stored

revolution NOUN
an attempt by a group of people to change their country's government by using force

rhythm NOUN
a regular pattern of sounds or movements

rock and roll NOUN
a type of music that was popular in the 1950s

role NOUN
the character that an actor plays in a film or a play

saxophone NOUN
a musical instrument made of metal that you play by blowing into it

state NOUN
a smaller area that some large countries such as the United States are divided into

step NOUN
one of a series of actions that you take in a process

street
on the streets PHRASE
without a home and having to sleep outside

studio NOUN
a room where people record music, or make radio or television programmes or films

successful ADJECTIVE
doing or getting what you wanted

talent NOUN
your natural ability to do something well

tango NOUN
a type of dance music originally from Argentina

tenor NOUN
a male singer with a fairly high voice

trombone NOUN
a metal musical instrument that you play by blowing into it and sliding part of it backwards and forwards

trouble
to get into trouble PHRASE
to be likely to be punished because you have broken a rule or law

trumpet NOUN
a musical instrument made of metal that you play by blowing into it

version NOUN
one form of something, for example a piece of music or a film, that is different from other forms of the same thing

Collins
English Readers

ALSO AVAILABLE IN THE AMAZING PEOPLE READERS SERIES:

Level 1

Amazing Leaders
978-0-00-754492-9
William the Conqueror, Saladin, Genghis Khan, Catherine the Great, Abraham Lincoln, Queen Victoria

Amazing Inventors
978-0-00-754494-3
Johannes Gutenberg, Louis Braille, Alexander Graham Bell, Thomas Edison, Guglielmo Marconi, John Logie Baird

Amazing Entrepreneurs and Business People
978-0-00-754501-8
Mayer Rothschild, Cornelius Vanderbilt, Will Kellogg, Elizabeth Arden, Walt Disney, Soichiro Honda

Amazing Women
978-0-00-754493-6
Harriet Tubman, Emmeline Pankhurst, Maria Montessori, Hellen Keller, Nancy Wake, Eva Peron

Level 2

Amazing Architects and Artists
978-0-00-754496-7
Leonardo da Vinci, Christopher Wren, Antoni Gaudí, Pablo Picasso, Frida Kahlo

Amazing Composers
978-0-00-754502-5
JS Bach, Wolfgang Mozart, Giuseppe Verdi, Johann Strauss, Pyotr Tchaikovsky, Irving Berlin

Amazing Aviators
978-0-00-754495-0
Joseph-Michel Montgolfier, Louis Blériot, Charles Lindbergh, Amelia Earhart, Amy Johnson

Amazing Mathematicians
978-0-00-754503-2
Galileo Galilei, René Descartes, Isaac Newton, Carl Gauss, Charles Babbage, Ada Lovelace

Amazing Medical People
978-0-00-754509-4
Edward Jenner, Florence Nightingale, Elizabeth Garrett, Carl Jung, Jonas Salk, Christiaan Barnard

Level 3

Amazing Explorers

978-0-00-754497-4

Marco Polo, Ibn Battuta, Christopher Columbus, James Cook, David Livingstone, Yuri Gagarin

Amazing Writers

978-0-00-754498-1

Geoffrey Chaucer, William Shakespeare, Charles Dickens, Victor Hugo, Leo Tolstoy, Rudyard Kipling

Amazing Philanthropists

978-0-00-754504-9

Alfred Nobel, Andrew Carnegie, John Rockefeller, Thomas Barnardo, Henry Wellcome, Madam CJ Walker

Amazing Performers

978-0-00-754505-6

Pablo Casals, Louis Armstrong, Édith Piaf, Frank Sinatra, Maria Callas, Elvis Presley

Amazing Scientists

978-0-00-754510-0

Antoine Lavoisier, Humphry Davy, Gregor Mendel, Louis Pasteur, Charles Darwin, Francis Crick

Level 4

Amazing Thinkers and Humanitarians

978-0-00-754499-8

Confucius, Socrates, Aristotle, William Wilberforce, Karl Marx, Mahatma Gandhi

Amazing Scientists

978-0-00-754500-1

Alessandro Volta, Michael Faraday, Marie Curie, Albert Einstein, Alexander Fleming, Linus Pauling

Amazing Writers

978-0-00-754506-3

Voltaire, Charlotte Brontë, Mark Twain, Jacques Prevert, Ayn Rand, Aleksandr Solzhenitsyn

Amazing Leaders

978-0-00-754507-0

Julius Caesar, Queen Elizabeth I, George Washington, King Louis XVI, Winston Churchill, Che Guevara

Amazing Entrepreneurs and Business People

978-0-00-754511-7

Henry Heinz, William Lever, Michael Marks, Henry Ford, Coco Chanel, Ray Kroc

Collins English Readers

Also available at this level

Level 1
CEF A2

Amazing Inventors
978-0-00-754494-3

Amazing Entrepreneurs and Business People
978-0-00-754501-8

Amazing Leaders
978-0-00-754492-9

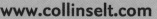

Amazing Women
978-0-00-754493-6

Sign up for our emails at **www.collinselt.com**
to receive free teaching and/or learning resources, as well as the most up-to-date news about new publications, events, and competitions.

POWERED BY COBUILD

www.collinselt.com   /collinselt   @CollinsELT